Building
DECKS

JOHN BOWLER

D1556067

MINI · WORKBOOK · SERIES

MURDOCH
B O O K S

CONTENTS

A deck with timber posts (top), deck stairs (far left) and a deck thoroughfare (left).

A deck provides a comfortable area for outdoor living, whether it is attached to the house or built in a sheltered corner of the garden.

Planning your deck

Careful planning and attention to the design before you start will make building your deck easier – and you'll end up with a deck that satisfies all your requirements.

WHY BUILD A DECK?

A deck extends your living area, providing a level area outside where you can sit comfortably. It is also practical as it will:

- compensate for sloping land;
- eliminate the problem of damp or shady areas where grass won't grow;
- increase the value of your house.

THE SIZE

The size of your deck will depend on the area available, its proposed function and, of course, your budget.

You may want to use the deck as:

- a place for children to play;
- an entertainment area;
- a place for outdoor barbecuing;
- a place to relax;
- a bridge or walkway;
- a surround for a pool, spa or children's sandpit.

A family of four to six people will generally need a deck approximately 12 m² to be comfortable. This will allow for a table and chairs but not a barbecue or plants. A safe estimate would be 2–2.5 m² per person.

THE LOCATION

The ideal location for a deck is on the southern side of the house where it will catch the summer sun. If this isn't possible, build it where it will be most useful. Note where shadows are cast on the ground as the sun moves through the sky from season to season. If necessary, add a screen or covered pergola to protect your deck from wind, rain or strong sun.

Other points to consider are:

- proximity to the house, especially the kitchen or family room;
- access to the garden;
- views;
- privacy (both your own and that of your neighbours).

TYPES OF DECKS

There are two main types of decks: attached and free-standing. An attached deck may be classified as a balcony or porch. It is fixed to the building for stability by means of a ledger, and so offers easy access to the house and its facilities.

A free-standing deck is an independent structure that supports itself. Instead of a ledger it has another row of posts. It is usually set away from the house but can be next to the house if you want to reduce the stress and load on the house and its footings. This type of deck is usually supported on brick piers or posts embedded in the ground. Posts supported in stirrups may be used, but these require additional bracing.

A free-standing deck can be built anywhere in the garden to take in a view, make better use of sloping land or surround a pool. It can be at ground level or raised, and it can be built in any shape, geometric or irregular. Walkways are essentially free-standing decks.

The basic elements of a deck are the same, whatever the type (see the diagram opposite).

DESIGNING A DECK

Once you have determined the function, size and location of your project, lay some timber around to mock up a full-size outline of the proposed deck. If you do not have timber available, use rope or even a garden hose to represent the outline.

Test out the area by positioning the tables, chairs or barbecue that will be used on the deck. Can you move around them comfortably? Will there be sufficient room to enjoy your deck? If not, you may need to increase the size or change the shape. However, keep in mind that bigger is not always better. Too big a deck could overpower the house and garden.

Be creative with your design, but keep it simple or it will be harder to build and will cost more. A split-level deck can make building on a steep site much easier, as it reduces the overall height of the construction. It also helps the deck to blend into the garden.

ACCESS

If you are attaching a deck to the house, consider how to ensure a smooth traffic flow from one to the other. Draw a plan of the rooms affected by the deck and map the traffic flow. You may need to move a door or replace a window with one (this should be done before the deck is built). A double-width door will allow the room inside to operate as an extension of the deck.

Decide whether you want stairs from the deck to the garden and where to locate them so they will provide a convenient entry.

ADDED FEATURES

Rocks or trees can be incorporated into the deck. Deciduous trees give shade in summer and let light in during winter. Allow room for the tree to grow and move with the wind. Lay temporary decking boards that can be removed as it grows.

Handrails and, perhaps, a pergola can be built as one with the deck by extending the posts up to the relevant height.

PREPARING PLANS

Once you have settled on a design, make some sketches of the deck with the dimensions on them. Discuss these with your local Building Control office before finalising the project to check whether there are restrictions. You may need to provide larger scale plans (with construction details) and obtain development and building approval before starting.

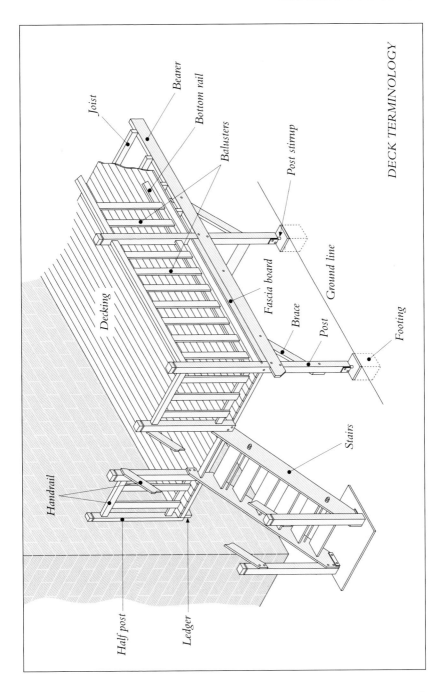

DECK TERMINOLOGY

Joist

Bearer

Bottom rail

Balusters

Post stirrup

Decking

Fascia board

Brace

Post

Ground line

Footing

Stairs

Handrail

Half post

Ledger

Choosing materials

Select the materials for your deck carefully, and it will last for many years. If timbers and hardware are not strong enough, the deck may actually be dangerous.

CHOOSING THE RIGHT TIMBER

The timber used for a deck will be exposed to all types of weather conditions and must be able to withstand them. With the increase in the numbers of wood-boring insects, it must also resist their attacks.

If you use unseasoned timber it will inevitably shrink, warp or bow. Most hardwood is only semi-seasoned when purchased, as fully seasoned hardwood is very difficult to work. However, most treated timber is seasoned.

When buying timber for your project, watch for faults such as bowing or twisting. Lightly bowed or twisted timber may be flattened or pulled straight while it is fixed into position. Badly affected timber may be unusable.

DURABILITY

Hardwoods have a high durability and can be used both in and out of the ground. However, it is recommended that any timber in direct contact with the ground be treated with a suitable preservative.

Any timber used in the ground will require a higher level of protection than that being used above the ground. There are various standards of rating timber for durability against the elements and resistance to attack. Any hardwood placed in the ground must have a high durability rating. Low-rated timber should not be used for weather-exposed structural members such as posts, bearers, joists or decking unless it has been pressure-treated.

PRESSURE-TREATED TIMBER

The most commonly used timbers for decks are pressure-treated softwoods such as the many varieties of pine. Preservative-treated softwoods are readily available from most timber merchants and are commonly treated with a compound of copper, chromium and arsenic, known as CCA. This gives the timber a characteristic green tone.

When using timber treated with CCA, wear gloves and a dust mask while sawing. Any cut or sawn surface of this material will need to be re-sealed to ensure its effectiveness in resisting attack. Dispose of any offcuts by burying them – do not burn them, as the smoke and ash created are toxic.

Commercially treated softwoods are available. These can be bought with a range of hazard levels from a

Using good-quality timbers with the appropriate durability and stress gradings will ensure your deck is strong and lasts for many years.

low to a high level of treatment. Brush-on preservative should be applied to all sawn or shaped surfaces.

Some treated timber may be water-repellent, but it will still weather, turning silvery grey over time. A decking oil or stain will counteract this, although it will require some maintenance.

Always take precautions when using treated timber:

• Always wear gloves when handling treated timber.
• Use a dust mask and goggles when machining, sawing or sanding.
• Ensure there is good ventilation in the work area.
• Wash your hands and face before drinking or eating.
• Wash work clothes separately.
• Never use treated timber for heating or cooking, especially on barbecues.

STRESS GRADINGS

Timber is also stress-graded. The 'C' rating is followed by a number, which indicates the bending stress. The higher the number the greater the stress it can withstand. Normally, bearers and joists should not be any less than C24; posts may be hardwood, C24 or greater if seasoned softwood. In the tables on pages 48 and 50 'oak' is used as a shorthand for 'hardwood' for reasons of space.

SPECIFICATIONS FOR DECK TIMBERS

The timber sizes suggested for use in the various parts of the deck (see the tables on pages 11–13) are a rough guide only. Consult your local Building Control office for details of the specifications required in your local area. Note that the standards in England and Wales are different from those in Scotland.

HARDWARE

Any deck is only as good as its fasteners, so make sure you always use good-quality fittings and fasteners that will stand the test of time.

Most fasteners and fittings are made from mild steel with a protective coating and, in most situations, hot-dipped galvanising is the preferred coating. Stainless-steel fasteners may be needed where there are high-corrosive conditions, such as decks built around salt-water pools or those built in areas subject to sea spray. Other metals such as brass and copper may be appropriate in some conditions, depending on the preservative used – check with your hardware supplier.

Machine or roundhead bolts hold structural members together far more strongly than nails. Coach screws may be used where access is restricted to one side. Washers should be used on both ends of machine bolts and also under the head of coach screws to prevent them from pulling too far into the timber.

Masonry anchors may be required to fix ledgers to brick walls, or stirrups to footings. Use the appropriate size of anchor – if the anchor is too short the device may

POST SIZES FOR DECKS

| | | Maximum height** | |
| | | Spacing between each post | |
Stress grade	Post size*	1800 mm	3600 mm
C16 unseasoned softwood	100 x 100 mm	3000 mm	2000 mm
	125 x 125 mm	4500 mm	3200 mm
C24 seasoned softwood	100 mm diameter	1900 mm	1300 mm
	90 x 90 mm/125 mm diameter	2700 mm	1900 mm
	150 mm diameter	4800 mm	3400 mm
Hardwood or better seasoned softwood	70 x 70 mm/100 mm diameter	2400 mm	2400 mm
	90 x 90 mm/125 mm diameter	3000 mm	2400 mm
	150 mm diameter	4800 mm	3700 mm

*When using sawn timber, increase the section size to the next largest, for example if using 90 x 90 mm, order 100 x 100 mm.
**Maximum height is taken from finished ground level.

DECK BEARER SIZES (SINGLE SPAN)

| | | Size of bearers (mm) | | |
| | | Maximum bearer span | | |
Stress grade	Joist span	1800 mm	2400 mm	3000 mm
C16 seasoned softwood	1800 mm	120 x 70	170 x 70	240 x 70
	2400 mm	140 x 70	190 x 70	240 x 70
	3000 mm	170 x 70	240 x 70	
C20 seasoned softwood	1800 mm	120 x 70	170 x 70	190 x 70
	2400 mm	120 x 70	170 x 70	240 x 70
	3000 mm	140 x 70	190 x 70	240 x 70
C24 seasoned softwood	1800 mm	120 x 70	170 x 70	190 x 70
	2400 mm	120 x 70	170 x 70	240 x 70
	3000 mm	140 x 70	170 x 70	240 x 70
	3600 mm	140 x 70	190 x70	240 x70

MAXIMUM JOIST SPAN (AND CANTILEVER) WITH JOISTS AT 450 mm CENTRES (mm)			
UNSEASONED TIMBER	C16	C24	HARDWOOD
150 x 50 mm	2800 (800)	2900 (800)	3400 (900)
175 x 50 mm	3000 (800)	3600 (1000)	3900 (1100)
200 x 50 mm	3800 (1100)	4000 (1100)	4300 (1200)
225 x 50 mm	4200 (1200)	4300 (1200)	
250 x 50 mm	4500 (1300)	4700 (1400)	
275 x 50 mm	4900 (1400)	5100 (1500)	
SEASONED TIMBER	C16	C24	HARDWOOD
140 x 45 mm	2600 (700)	2600 (700)	3100 (900)
190 x 45 mm	3500 (900)	3700 (1000)	3900 (1100)

not hold tight; if it is too thin it may snap when subjected to stress.

The decking itself is subject to constant movement as it expands and contracts according to the weather, and as people walk over it. Galvanised nails with a spiral or twisted shank are best for fixing it, as lost-head (bullet-head) plain-shank nails do not have as much holding power. Lost-head nails are satisfactory for the framework.

There are special decking screws available with countersunk heads, but

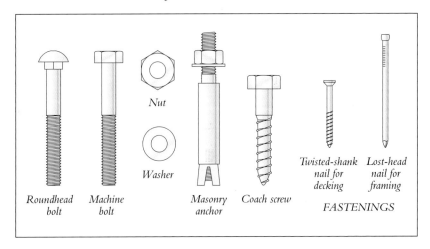

Roundhead bolt   *Machine bolt*   *Nut*   *Washer*   *Masonry anchor*   *Coach screw*   *Twisted-shank nail for decking*   *Lost-head nail for framing*

FASTENINGS

MAXIMUM JOIST SPAN (AND CANTILEVER) WITH JOISTS AT 600 mm CENTRES (mm)

Unseasoned timber	C16	C24	Hardwood
150 x 50 mm	2700 (700)	2800 (800)	3100 (900)
175 x 50 mm	3200 (900)	3300 (1000)	3600 (1000)
200 x 50 mm	3600 (1000)	3700 (1000)	4000 (1100)
225 x 50 mm	3900 (1100)	4000 (1200)	
250 x 50 mm	4200 (1200)	4400 (1300)	
275 x 50 mm	4500 (1300)	4700 (1400)	
300 x 50 mm	4900 (1400)	5000 (1400)	
Seasoned timber	C16	C24	Hardwood
140 x 45 mm	2500 (600)	2500 (700)	2900 (900)
190 x 45 mm	3200 (900)	3500 (1000)	3600 (1000)

they are only needed under extreme conditions. A well-nailed deck will normally give long service.

Other metal timber connectors, such as nail plates, frame connectors and joist hangers, are made from galvanised steel. There are many different types of connectors and they can be used for scores of different applications.

Post stirrups, or supports, and brackets (see the diagram on page 14)

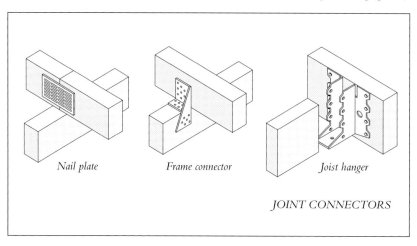

Nail plate   Frame connector   Joist hanger

JOINT CONNECTORS

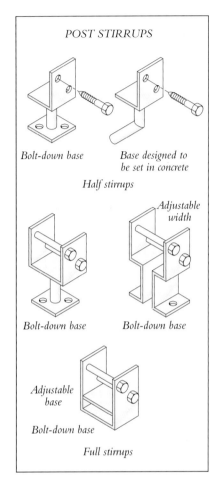

POST STIRRUPS

Bolt-down base

Base designed to
be set in concrete

Half stirrups

*Adjustable
width*

Bolt-down base

Bolt-down base

*Adjustable
base*

Bolt-down base

Full stirrups

help when you come to estimate the materials required for building your deck. Mistakes at this stage can be costly, as timber is expensive.

Use the materials and tools lists opposite to make a checklist of all that you will need to suit your deck. This will also help you cost the deck.

ORDERING MATERIALS

Most timber merchants will help you to order the correct quantities, grades and species of timber for your project – just show them the plan.

Timber is sold in set lengths, starting at 1.8 m and increasing in multiples of 300 mm. It may not be possible for a supplier to hold every length. Therefore, you may need to combine different measurements to avoid waste. For example, if 1.8 m joists are required and the supplier's lengths start at 2.4 m, there would be 600 mm of waste from each joist. However, the supplier may have 3.6 m lengths, in which case two joists could be obtained from each.

Decking may be purchased by the square or linear metre. Allow at least 10 per cent waste for cutting.

STORING TIMBER

When timber is delivered to the job, remember to keep it off the ground to prevent it being affected by rising moisture. Always keep it covered to protect it from rain. Moisture can cause the timber to warp or split. Keep the stack out of the way so it doesn't interfere with the smooth flow of the job.

are hot-dipped galvanised by the manufacturer. If they are cut or drilled for any reason, reapply a protective coat of galvanised paint.

ESTIMATING MATERIALS

The plans for the deck that you have drawn up to submit to your local authority for approval, will probably have to include detailed specifications and dimensions. These drawings will

MATERIALS CHECKLIST

Timber (specify type and size)

- Posts (or steel posts or bricks for piers)
- Ledger
- Bearers
- Joists
- Decking
- Handrailing
- Balusters
- Stair strings
- Stair treads
- Fascia boards
- Bracing
- Temporary bracing or props

Other

- Concrete for footings
- Flashing

- Drainage pipes, gravel, landscape fabric (weed mat)
- Galvanised post stirrups or brackets
- Galvanised bolts
- Capping (for brick piers)
- Galvanised bolts/coach screws with washers (for fixing bearer to post, ledger to wall, handrail to deck)
- Masonry anchors
- Lost-head galvanised nails: 100 x 3.75 mm, 75 x 3.5 mm for construction
- Twisted-shank decking nails: 50 x 3.5 mm
- Framing brackets (joist hangers)
- Nail plates
- Tie rods for stairs
- Oil finishes or stains (primers, filler, finish coats)

TOOLS

- Builders square
- Chalk line
- Chisels
- Circular saw
- Combination square
- Cramps
- Crowbar
- Electric drill and bits

- Electric plane
- Excavation machinery★
- Hammer
- Hand saw
- Nail punch
- Plumb bob
- Pneumatic nail gun and compressor★

- Post-hole shovel or auger★
- Shovel
- Spanner
- Spirit level
- String line
- Tape measure
- Water level

★ Can be hired if necessary.

Getting started

Before you begin building your deck you will need to prepare the site and set out the area for construction.

PREPARING THE SITE

If necessary, level the site, although the post heights can be adjusted to allow for uneven ground.

DRAINAGE

If you are building on clayey soil or the site is subjected to a lot of water, use a rubble drain to divert it away from the structure. The drain should be connected to an absorption pit or stormwater pipe out on to the street. It should not direct water onto a neighbouring property.

To construct a rubble drain, dig a trench around the area, allowing for a slight fall to the stormwater pipe or pit. Dig the trench 50 mm deeper than the bottom of the footing. Place 75 mm of coarse gravel or river stone in the bottom of the trench. Lay a plastic agricultural drainage pipe (slotted PVC pipe, preferably with a fine nylon screen sock over it) on top and cover it with fine gravel. Cover this with a landscape fabric (weed mat) and a layer of soil.

WEED CONTROL

Ideally, remove the top layer of soil to ensure grass and weeds don't grow through the deck. The area can also be covered with a landscape fabric and 50 mm of medium gravel. This will also help to drain the surface.

THE LEDGER

When building an attached deck, first fix the ledger to the house, tying the frame of the deck to the building and its solid foundation. The ledger must be secured at the correct height and it must be level. The height depends on whether the joists will be placed on top of it or against its face.

FIXING THE LEDGER

1 Determine the height for the top of the ledger. Allow for the thickness of the decking (usually 22 mm) and the height of the joists, if applicable. The decking should lie 25 mm below any sill, so that rainwater won't run back into the house. Use a spirit level and straight edge, or a water level and chalk line, to mark out the top of the ledger on the side of the house.

2 If the house has weatherboards, remove one or two to provide a flat surface for the ledger. Place flashing directly above the ledger to prevent water entering the house, and fit a timber spacer behind the ledger so the full width of the ledger will support the joists.

3 Use coach screws to attach the ledger to the house frame or bolt it through to the bearer or joists. Drill

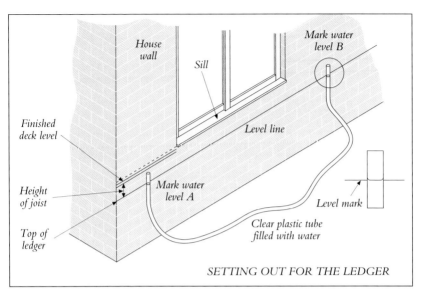

SETTING OUT FOR THE LEDGER

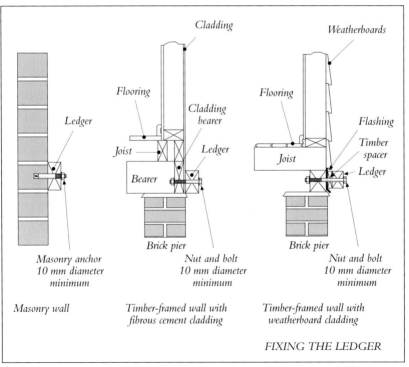

Masonry anchor
10 mm diameter
minimum

Masonry wall

Nut and bolt
10 mm diameter
minimum

*Timber-framed wall with
fibrous cement cladding*

Nut and bolt
10 mm diameter
minimum

*Timber-framed wall with
weatherboard cladding*

FIXING THE LEDGER

holes through the ledger for the screws, directly below where each alternate deck joist will be.

4 Hold the ledger at its correct location against the house and check that it is level. Insert a pencil through the drilled holes and mark the wall. You may need a helper or temporary props to hold the work, as accuracy is important. Insert screws or bolts.

SETTING OUT AN ATTACHED DECK

5 Tack a nail into the top of the ledger at one end. Then, tie a string line to the nail and square off the house by placing a builders square on the ground. At least one arm of the square must be level. This will give you a rough line for erecting the building profile. Measure out along this line 600 mm more than the required location of the posts.

6 Construct a building profile using pointed pegs and a horizontal cross-piece 600 mm long (see diagram opposite). The pegs must be strong enough to support the stretched

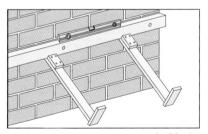

4 *Use temporary props to hold the ledger at its correct location against the house and check that it is level.*

string. If the deck is too high for the profile, fix a temporary ledger (batten) to the wall while you are setting out. This should be about 300 mm above the ground, level and parallel to the ledger. Place the top of the profile in the same horizontal plane as the ledger. Remove the temporary string line.

7 Using the '3-4-5' method, square the string line off the house at the end of the ledger. Fix the string line to the profile at this position. Repeat at the other end of the ledger.

8 Erect profiles parallel to each string line and 600 mm outside them. Set up the string line for the posts by measuring the required distance from the house along the string lines. Stretch a third string line across and tie it to the outside profiles.

9 Check the string lines are parallel and at the same slope, and measure the diagonals. If they are equal, the set-out is square. Adjust as required. Attach the string line to a small nail in the top of the profile; check again.

SETTING OUT A FREE-STANDING DECK

Free-standing decks have an extra row of posts and a bearer instead of a ledger. Drive in pegs at the corners on the high side of the area. Use a string line and level to bring them to a level plane. Set out the other sides as for the attached deck, using the level line instead of the ledger.

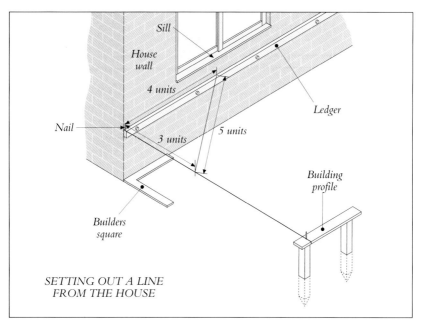

Sill

House wall

4 units

Ledger

Nail

5 units

3 units

Building profile

Builders square

SETTING OUT A LINE FROM THE HOUSE

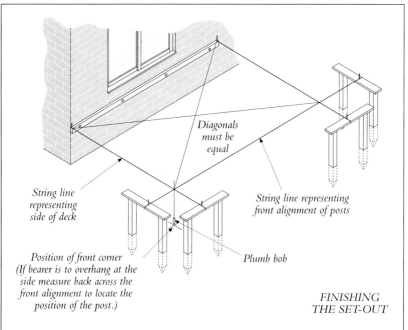

Diagonals must be equal

String line representing side of deck

String line representing front alignment of posts

Position of front corner (If bearer is to overhang at the side measure back across the front alignment to locate the position of the post.)

Plumb bob

FINISHING THE SET-OUT

The footings for this deck are concealed by attractive trellis work, which complements the arches at the top of the posts.

Footings and posts

Footings and posts provide the basic support for the deck. The posts must be strong enough to bear its weight, and the footings should be spaced correctly to make the structure solid.

FOOTINGS

A footing (normally made of concrete) is placed in the ground to stabilise the deck structure. The footing must rest on solid ground capable of carrying the load of the deck safely without any undue movement. Depending on the type of soil at your site, the size of the footing will vary (consult your local Building Control office).

If you are using timber posts, the height of the concrete footing is not important. However, the top should be approximately 50 mm above the ground and the surface graded away from the post or its support. This helps to prevent the water from welling around the post. If a timber post is to be placed in the footing, 75 mm of coarse gravel (approximately 20 mm in diameter) should be placed in the bottom of the hole.

If the deck is to rest on brick piers the footings usually finish below ground level. The precise height will depend on the pier, which must be an even number of brick courses and finish immediately below the bearer.

MAKING THE FOOTINGS

1 Set out the site (see pages 16–19). Use a permanent marker to mark the location of each post on the string line. The spacing for the posts will depend on the section, size and grade of timber used for the bearer (see table on page 11). The standard

FOOTINGS FOR BRACED DECKS*	
AREA SUPPORTED BY EACH POST**	MINIMUM FOOTING SIZE
5 m^2	300 x 300 mm; 600 mm deep
10 m^2	600 x 600 mm; 600 mm deep
15 m^2	600 x 600 mm; 600 mm deep
20 m^2	750 x 750 mm; 600 mm deep

*Suitable for decks up to 3.6 m above ground on minimum soil-bearing pressure of 150 kPa, such as rock, sand or gravel of medium density, or moderately stiff clay.

**This can be calculated by multiplying the bearer span by the joist span.

spacing is 1.8 m although this may increase to 3.6 m. Using a plumb bob or spirit level, transfer these positions to the ground. This mark will represent the centre front alignment for each pier or post. Use a peg to indicate the centre of each post and remove the string line.

2 Determine the size of the footings (see the table on page 21).

3 The bottom of the footing must rest on stable ground, so remove any tree roots. Remove the top layer of dirt with a garden spade and use a post-hole shovel or auger to dig the footing holes. Hold the handles together and drive the blades into the ground a few times to break up the soil. Spread the handles to hold the soil, then lift it out and place the dirt far enough away from the excavation to avoid any falling back into the hole. (If there is a large number of holes, you can hire a powered post-hole auger; be sure to get adequate instructions from the hire company.)

4 Construct a 100 mm high timber form box and place it over the hole, centred on the post position. Fix it with pegs – you may need to brace it temporarily to hold it in the correct location. Paint the inside of the formwork with a little oil – this makes it easier to remove once the concrete has set.

5 The concrete mix should not be too wet. The consistency should be wet enough to pour, yet stiff enough to hold the post or stirrups until set. Pour the concrete mix into the form and ram it down well with a piece of timber to prevent air pockets, as they will hold water and can cause the post to rot or rust.

DIGGING IN SOFT SOIL

If you have sandy or soft soil that tends to fall into the hole as you dig, then cut the top and bottom from a 23 litre drum. Place the drum in position and dig through it. Push it into the excavation as you go. This drum may also be used as formwork when you are pouring the wet concrete for the footing.

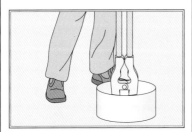

To stop sandy soil falling into the hole as you dig, place a drum in position and dig through it.

POSTS OR PIERS

Generally, decks are supported by posts, or by piers or columns. Timber or steel posts are the more common method of support, and they can be either round or square. Steel posts are embedded into the concrete footing while timber posts may be placed in the footing or on post stirrups (supports). Posts may extend through the top of the deck to provide support for a handrail or even a pergola (roof).

Timber posts should have a C24 stress rating if they are hardwood and at least C24 if treated softwood (see pages 8–10). For suitable timber sizes see the table on page 11. When softwood posts will be embedded in the ground, use timber with a high rating (check with your local authority about conditions in your area). Ensure you place the trimmed end up so that it is above ground level and the end in the ground is the one fully treated by the supplier. You can use brush-on preservatives but they do not have the same amount of penetration as pressure-treatment.

Piers or columns are normally made of brickwork or from reinforced concrete poured into a form tube. For high-wind areas a tie-down rod must be placed in the columns and embedded into the footing during construction.

If necessary, packing such as fibrous cement sheets can be placed on top of the pier to get the precise height for the bearer. The external face of the pier should align with the string line. On top of each pier place a damp-proof course and, particularly in areas where insects are a problem, capping. Brick piers and footings must comply with current building standards and codes.

For a narrow attached deck with ledger, only one bearer and one row of posts are required. For a free-

A metal stirrup supports this timber post, raising it and protecting it from rot and insect attack.

standing deck you need a minimum of two bearers and two rows of posts. Extra bearers and rows of posts will have to be added to make a larger deck.

ERECTING THE POSTS

1 If stirrups are to be embedded in the footing, place them in the wet concrete, ensuring they are aligned with the string line. Use a level to

HINT

Check with your local authorities for the location of underground services such as gas or water pipes, phone or electric cables. If you damage them you may not only have to pay the repair cost, but you may be placing yourself in danger.

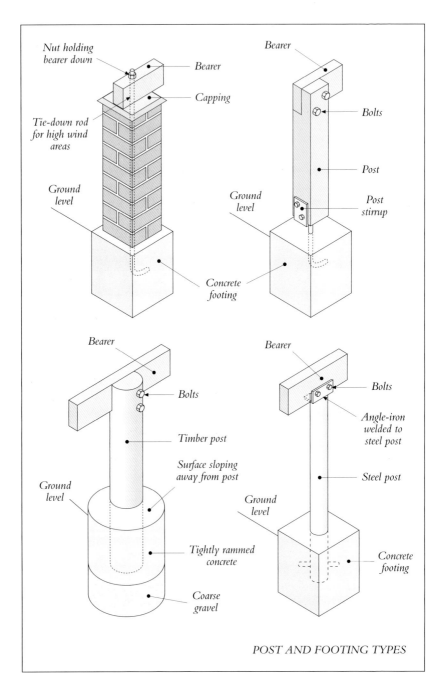

Nut holding bearer down

Bearer

Capping

Tie-down rod for high wind areas

Ground level

Concrete footing

Bearer

Bolts

Post

Post stirrup

Ground level

Bearer

Bolts

Timber post

Surface sloping away from post

Ground level

Tightly rammed concrete

Coarse gravel

Bearer

Bolts

Angle-iron welded to steel post

Steel post

Ground level

Concrete footing

POST AND FOOTING TYPES

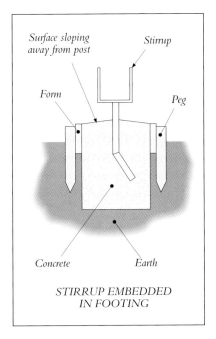

Surface sloping away from post

Stirrup

Form

Peg

Concrete

Earth

STIRRUP EMBEDDED IN FOOTING

concrete is set. Timber posts can be cut to height after the concrete has set. Steel posts must be set in the concrete at the correct height, as they cannot be cut later. The string line should align with the position of the lower edge of the bearer or its housing. Finally, allow the concrete footings to cure for approximately seven days before continuing.

2 If you are using bolt-down stirrups, fix them in place. Take one post and stand it in a stirrup in its correct alignment with the string line. It should be a little longer than the finished post to allow for fitting and levelling. Temporarily fix the post with one nail or screw through the holes in the stirrup. This will hold the base of the post and leave the top free. Use a spirit level to check for vertical both ways and temporarily brace the post. Repeat this for the post at the opposite end and for any intermediate posts. Again, check that the posts are vertical and in alignment, and adjust them as required.

check the alignment. Alternatively, embed a treated timber or steel post in the concrete. The posts may need to be temporarily braced in position while the concrete is poured and setting. They must be perfectly vertical and in alignment, as there is no easy way to correct this once the

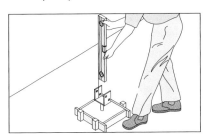

1 Place a stirrup in the wet concrete, ensuring it is aligned with the string line. Use a level to check alignment.

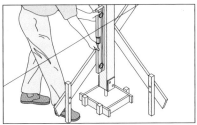

2 Stand a post in the stirrup, aligning it with the string line. Fix it temporarily with a nail or screw.

The ends of the joists here have been painted to match the bearer and bottom railing so that they create a decorative checked effect. A fascia board could have been used to conceal them.

The horizontal framework

A deck is a simple structure similar to the interior floor of a house. Bearers rest on the posts and joists on the bearers, thus making the horizontal framework for the deck.

TIMBER

Bearers and joists are usually of medium durability or greater, and are of pressure-treated timber (see pages 8–10). They should have a stress rating of no less than C24. For suitable sizes, see the tables on pages 11–13.

BEARERS

The bearers span from post-to-post. In the case of an attached deck, the decking boards and bearers usually run parallel to the house and the ledger. For example, if you want the decking boards to run at 90 degrees from the house, you can fix the bearers to the top of the ledger at the same angle.

Bearers can be fixed to the posts in a number of ways:

• They can be housed into the posts below the level line (see pages 28–9).

• They can sit on top of the posts and be fixed with skew-nailing or, preferably, nail plates.

• Bearers can be bolted directly into the face of the post.

If desired, a pair of bearers can be attached to either side of the post with solid blocking between. In this case smaller timber sections can be used. Take care to ensure that the top edges of both bearers are at the same level and alignment, or they won't support the joists properly.

DETERMINING THE BEARER HEIGHT

Take care in determining the bearer height and levels, as you don't want a twisted, uneven or out-of-level deck. Check again that the posts are aligned and vertical, and transfer a level mark from the top of the ledger to each post. For wider decks use a water level, but on narrower decks a straight edge and spirit level may be used. Rest the spirit level in the centre of the straight edge. With one end of the straight edge resting on top of the ledger, move the other up or down until the edge is level. Mark the bottom of the straight edge on the post.

• If the joists are to be fixed on top of the ledger and bearer, this will become the top of the bearer. Transfer the mark onto all the corner posts. Pull a string line tightly from each corner post and mark the bearer height on each intermediate post.

• If the joists are to be fixed at the height of the ledger but over the bearers, the bearer will need to be lower. Measure down the height of the joists from the original mark.

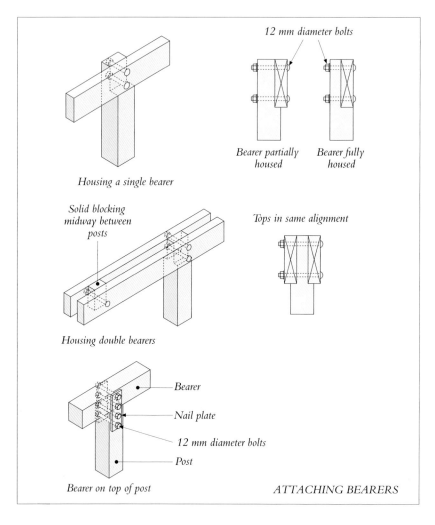

12 mm diameter bolts

Housing a single bearer

Bearer partially housed

Bearer fully housed

Solid blocking midway between posts

Tops in same alignment

Housing double bearers

Bearer

Nail plate

12 mm diameter bolts

Post

Bearer on top of post

ATTACHING BEARERS

Then, make a second mark and transfer it to all of the posts in the same way.

If bearers are not long enough and have to be joined end-to-end, the joint must be placed directly over a post. In the case of double bearers, the joins should be staggered. Use a scarf joint for maximum strength.

ATTACHING THE BEARERS

1 If the posts are in stirrups, number each post and stirrup to match (the post heights may vary). Place a cross on the side of the post where the bearer is to be fitted. Remove the posts from the stirrups and lay each one on a set of trestles so that you can work on them easily.

This bearer is housed into the posts, which continue up to support the railing.

2 The bearers are housed into the posts below the level line. From the line on each post measure down the height of the bearer. Square both lines across the face and down each side. Mark the depth of the housing: it is generally the thickness of the bearers or a maximum of two-thirds the thickness of the post. Cut the housings with a power saw. Clean them out with a chisel and check that they fit neatly.

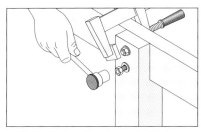

4 Drill bolt holes through the bearer into the post, apply preservative and fasten with the bolts.

3 Re-erect each post in its correct location and check that it is in alignment and vertical. Use braces to hold it in position. Fasten it to the stirrup with 10 mm bolts.

4 Place the bearer in position. Level it and secure it with a cramp. Use galvanised cuphead bolts (preferably two per post). Drill the bolt holes through the bearer into the post. The drill bit may not be long enough to go through the bearer and the post; if so, remove the bearer and continue to drill the holes all the way through. Apply a coat of preservative to both surfaces within the joint. Replace the bearer and fasten with the bolts.

JOISTS

Joists span the width of the deck and are fixed to the bearer and ledger, or two bearers, in one of several ways:

• Joists may sit on top of the bearers, and be skew-nailed or fixed with a frame connector.

• Joists may sit against the face of the bearers and ledger. Use joist hangers for maximum strength.

• Joists may fit against the face of the ledger and over the bearers.

Other types of framing brackets may also be used. If you are using joist hangers, the ledger, bearers and joist should be the same size.

The joists may finish at, or extend past, the outside bearer. Allowing them to overhang the bearer will make the deck more attractive as the posts will be set back from the edge.

The posts will also be less noticeable, especially if they are camouflaged by plants. The overhang must not exceed one-quarter of the joist span (see the diagram opposite).

Although joists are usually laid at right angles to bearers this can vary, for example if you are laying decking boards in a pattern (see page 36).

ATTACHING JOISTS

1 Mark the spacings for each joist on top of the ledger and bearers by measuring along both from the same end. This will ensure that the joists are parallel, whether or not the spacings between them are even. The

---

FIXING TO A ROUND POST

1 To house a bearer into a round post, first measure the thickness of the bearer back from the front edge. Then mark this thickness across the top of each post, measuring from the front. Pull a string line across the top of the row of posts to represent the back of the housing.

2 Draw a vertical line down each side of the post the height of the bearer. Use a square piece of cardboard as a guide and mark a line around the post.

3 Cut the housing with a hand saw for safety and remove the waste with a chisel.

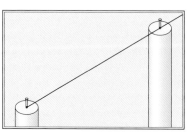

1 Measure the thickness of the bearer back from the front edge and pull a string line across the posts.

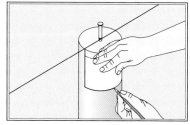

2 Use a square piece of cardboard to mark the line for the bottom of the housing around the post.

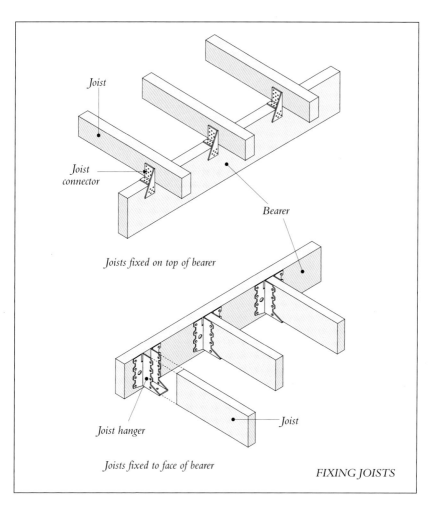

Joist

Joist connector

Bearer

Joists fixed on top of bearer

Joist hanger

Joist

Joists fixed to face of bearer

FIXING JOISTS

maximum recommended spacing will not always suit your deck. You can either adjust it and keep all the spacing the same, or adjust the two end spaces only. Never exceed the maximum recommended spacing (see the tables on pages 12–13).

2 Square the spacings down the face of the ledger and place a cross to mark the position of the joist. Using galvanised 30 x 2.8 mm clout nails or those recommended by the manufacturer, fix one side of the hanger to the ledger or bearer. Position it so that the joist and ledger are flush on top. Use an offcut of joist material to help position the hanger (this will be easier than manoeuvring a joist).

Wood preserve is an excellent insect repellent and is used on the underside of decks or around the bottom of posts that are placed in the ground. Care must be exercised when using this product. Be sure to follow the manufacturer's instructions.

3 Square the ledger end of the two outside joists. Do not cut them to finished length unless they are to fit between the ledger and the bearer. If they sit over the bearer they are trimmed later. Apply a preservative and fit the joist in the hanger. Fix the other side of the hanger to the ledger and then fix it to the joist. If the joists sit on top of the ledger, leave a 10 mm gap between the end of the joist and the wall.

4 Check that the posts are still vertical and aligned. Skew-nail the other end of the joist to the top of the bearer with one 75 x 3.5 mm galvanised nail, or temporarily fix a hanger in place.

5 Measure the diagonals of the structure for square and adjust as required. You may need to use a temporary brace to hold the structure square. When you are satisfied, finish fixing the end joists and all those remaining, keeping any bows in the timber at the top.

6 If the joists overhang, mark the required length on each end joist and stretch a string line between them. Draw vertical lines down the sides of each one to correspond with the string line, and cut them to length.

FINISHING THE FRAMEWORK

7 If desired, fix a fascia board over the ends of the joists to give the deck a neater finish. The board must be well secured if a handrail is to be attached to it.

8 Fix any necessary bracing (see the box opposite). Once these braces are permanently fixed, any temporary bracing that was used to hold the structure square during construction may be removed.

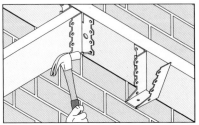

3 Fix one side of the hanger to the ledger, square the end of the joist, then fix the other side of the hanger.

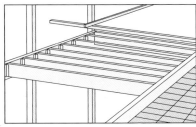

5 Fix temporary braces to hold the structure square and finish fixing the joists in position.

BRACING THE DECK

A deck that is securely fixed to a house, especially in a corner, will require only minimal bracing, if any. A deck higher than 1200 mm should have at least a pair of opposing braces. Decks higher than 1800 mm and wider than 2000 mm need a pair of opposing braces in both directions. Any deck built in a high-wind area or that is free-standing on stirrups should also be braced.

A simple 100 x 50 mm timber brace at 45 degrees (from post to bearer and secured with bolts) will be adequate in most situations. The brace angle may vary up to 5 degrees, but the bottom of the brace should not be lower than half the post height.

For taller or free-standing decks, cross-bracing from the top of one post to the bottom of the next will provide better stability.

The bracing will not necessarily detract from the appearance of the deck, as it can be concealed with lattice, vertical or horizontal battens or a trellis for a climbing vine. Fix the diagonal bracing under the joists with halving joints in the centre. Use 90 x 45 mm timbers and bolt them at each end with a 12 mm diameter bolt. Nail them to each joist.

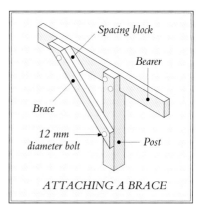

ATTACHING A BRACE

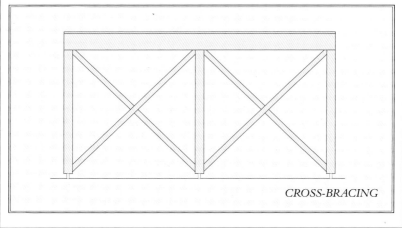

CROSS-BRACING

33

The decking

The decking is the part of a deck most often seen, and so selection of the timber and accurate fixing is a crucial part of building such a structure.

DECKING BOARDS

The decking boards are fixed on top of the joists parallel to the bearers. They must be spaced a little apart to allow water to pass through.

Decking boards come in various sizes, the two most common being machined from 100 x 25 mm or 75 x 25 mm timber. They are suitable for 450 mm joist spacings. Other sizes may be machined to order.

Decking is subjected to weather and traffic and so must be good quality timber. Use either seasoned hardwood with medium durability or treated softwood with a medium rating or greater. Decking should be free of structural defects, especially splits and knots. Cup-faced boards should be laid with the cup down to prevent anyone tripping on them.

Most timber suppliers will have a selection of decking boards, varying in durability, grading, shapes and, of course, price. Decking is usually purchased by the square or lineal metre; allow 10 per cent for wastage.

Don't use short lengths: the boards must span at least three joists. Fluted or skid-resistant boards are best as they are attractive and make the gaps between boards less obvious. They should be used around pools.

The most commonly used decking profiles have rounded top edges that are splinter-free, more even to walk on and accept stain more readily.

HINT
Add a coat of preservative or stain before the boards are nailed down. It's also a good idea to apply a coat to the tops of joists and other hard-to-reach spots.

DECKING SPANS★		
	THICKNESS	MAXIMUM JOIST SPACING
Hardwood	19 mm	500 mm
	25 mm	650 mm
Treated softwood	22 mm	450 mm
★ Standard-grade timbers. The spans for different designs are given in the diagram on page 36.		

Decking boards should be securely fixed and properly spaced to provide a safe and comfortable floor for a deck.

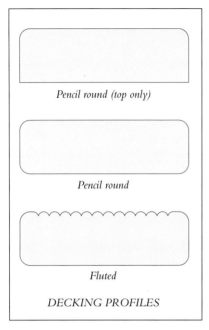

Pencil round (top only)

Pencil round

Fluted

DECKING PROFILES

DECKING PATTERNS

Decking is usually laid parallel to the house, but laying it at different angles can give a more interesting effect. This takes longer and costs more, but the result will be well worth it.

If you are laying a pattern, the placement and direction of the joists will need to be worked out to accommodate it. To ensure a solid surface where decking is joined, use double joists. The joist spacing should be calculated in the direction in which the decking is to be laid, not square off the joists.

LAYING THE DECKING

1 Cut the tops of all the joists flush and remove any bows that project too high. Check the frame with a

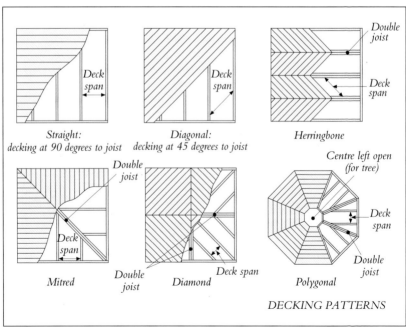

Straight:
decking at 90 degrees to joist

Diagonal:
decking at 45 degrees to joist

Herringbone

Mitred

Diamond

Polygonal

DECKING PATTERNS

long straight edge and trim the tops of the joists with a power plane.

2 Select the straightest decking board to start with, as this will determine the position of all the others. Allow the board to extend past the finished length (it will be trimmed later). The deck will look better if it has a 10–25 mm overhang on all outside edges (see the diagram on page 38). To determine the placement of the first board, subtract the overhang from the width of the board. Therefore, a board of 66 mm width with an overhang on the outside edge of 10 mm will have a starter width of 56 mm. Measure in 56 mm from the outside edge at both ends and stretch and snap a chalk line between these two points. This will provide a straight line to start on.

3 Secure the first board in line with the chalk mark. Using twisted-shank nails (see page 12), nail from one end to the other, straightening the board as you go. Drive in two nails per joist at a slight angle and punch the heads below the surface.

● If there are handrail posts you may have to secure the first board further in from the edge to clear the posts. In this case, the starting position should match equal board widths and gaps from the outside. The decking can be cut in around the posts later.
● At the ends of the boards drill pilot holes to prevent them from splitting. Drill the pilot hole slightly smaller than the nail diameter. You may also need to drill holes through the decking if the timber is too dry and likely to split.
● To save time, you can use a powered nail gun. Ensure the nails are suitable for use in the gun.

4 Scatter a number of boards on the joist at a time to provide a work platform. Position the next board against the first board with its end extending past the finished length. It will be trimmed off later. Leave a small gap (3–4 mm) between the boards for drainage and to allow dirt to fall through. (This gap may seem small, but the timber will shrink over time.) A nail can be used as a spacer to maintain the gap. Use a spacer at

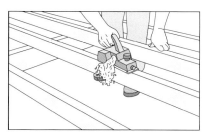

1 Check the frame with a long straight edge and trim the tops of the joists with a power plane.

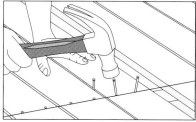

4 Use a nail as a spacer and drive in two nails per joist at a slight angle. Punch the heads below the surface.

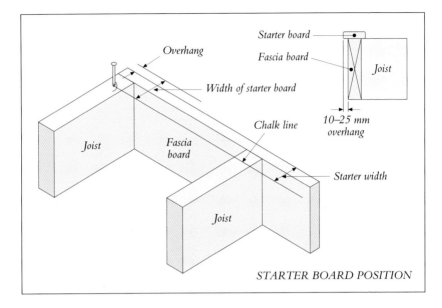

STARTER BOARD POSITION

one end and another in close proximity to the joist that the decking is being nailed to. Nail the boards down as for the first board.

5 Straighten bowed decking boards as you work.
• If the board bows in, nail one end in place. Work along the board, placing the spacer to create the required gap. At the bow, drive a

chisel into the top of the joist and lever the board over to the spacer. Nail down. Continue this from joist-to-joist. Look along the board to check for straightness.
• If the board is bowed out, secure each end with the correct spacing. Then, place a spacer in the centre of the bow. Use the chisel to lever the board over and nail. Repeat this on both sides of each joist. Check the

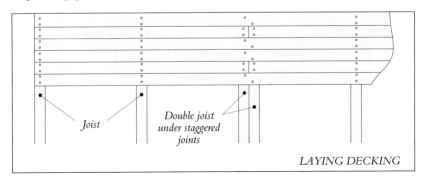

LAYING DECKING

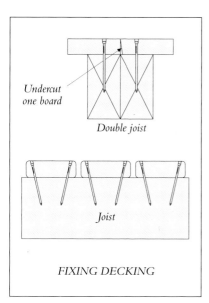

Undercut one board

Double joist

Joist

FIXING DECKING

the remaining gaps slightly to make any adjustment.

7 Stagger joins, and if possible support them on double joists. To obtain a tight fit, one of the ends can be undercut slightly.

TRIMMING DECKING ENDS

8 Mark the overhang at each end of the deck, that is on the first and last boards. Measure the distance from the blade of your circular saw to the outside edge of the base plate. Mark this distance in from the overhang position and secure a straight edge as a guide for the saw to run against. Look along the guide and straighten it if required by nailing at regular intervals. Alternatively, snap a chalk line between the two overhang points and cut along this line. However, this method does require greater accuracy in use of the saw.

9 Place the circular saw against the straight edge and trim the overhang. Round over the trimmed ends with a hand plane or router. Sand the boards if required.

board for straightness and continue the process as required.

6 Regularly check the decking for parallel, especially the remaining spacing. Measure at each end and in the centre. If the spacing is not parallel, adjust the gaps over the next few boards and re-check the measurements. To avoid finishing with uneven boards or spacing, check your measurements on the last 900 mm or so. Then, open or close

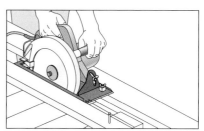

8 Trim the ends of the decking boards using a circular saw with a straight edge nailed to the deck as a guide.

HINT

When using a nail as a spacer, drive it through a piece of thin timber to prevent it repeatedly falling between the boards. Use three spacers – one at each end and one where you are working.

Stairs are essential to provide easy access to the garden from any deck apart from those right on ground level.

Deck stairs

Whether the deck is attached or free-standing, it will in most cases need stairs for access to the garden and perhaps between levels. A basic open stair is all that is needed.

DESIGNING DECK STAIRS

Stairs for a deck should not be elaborate, as fine detailing can trap moisture and cause rot. Use a concrete pad or footings under the strings to keep them above the ground and away from moisture.

A comfortable width for a stair is about 900 mm and it should not be less than 760 mm. If it is wider than 900 mm it will require a string (centre carriage piece) for support.

The string tops can be fixed by one of two methods (see page 44):

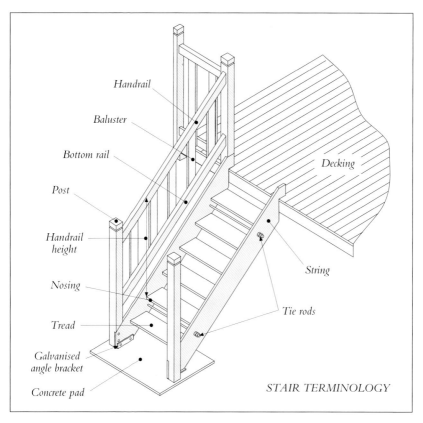

Handrail

Baluster

Bottom rail

Post

Handrail height

Nosing

Tread

Galvanised angle bracket

Concrete pad

Decking

String

Tie rods

STAIR TERMINOLOGY

• cutting hooks in the end of the string to sit on the joist or decking;
• cutting the end to fit against the face of the joist and holding it in place with a ledger or angle brackets.

PARTS OF THE STAIRS

• Strings. These are the main support for the stairs. There is one on each side spanning from the deck to the ground. The treads are attached to them. Strings may have a sawtooth shape or a straight top. The timber used should be as straight as possible and free from any defects.

• Treads. These are the steps. To create a horizontal surface to walk on, they are attached to strings on both sides, either the top of sawtoothed strings or the face of the strings. They can be housed into the string or secured to them on timber supports or steel brackets (see page 45). Two pieces of timber laid side-by-side to obtain the required tread width are better than one wide piece, as wider pieces are more prone to distortion when exposed to the weather. The nosing is the front of the tread and the going is the clear tread width.

• Riser. This is the vertical distance between the top of one tread and the the next (the height of each step). Internal stairs may have a riser board placed between the treads but this is not common on external stairs. The total 'rise' is the effective height of all the risers added together.

Your local Building Control office will have regulations for building stairs and these will ensure that you construct a comfortable and safe stairway. Some of the regulations in the Building Regulations (1991) (Part K) include:

• All the rise measurements in the stairway must be the same and measure between 220 and 115 mm.

• Treads must have a clear width of between 220 and 355 mm.

• The relation between tread and risers must be such that:

$2R + G$ = between 550 and 700 mm
(where R = riser and G = going or clear tread width)

The regulations also state that a stair over 600 mm in height or more than five risers must have a handrail not less than 900 mm high.

MEASURING UP

1 To determine the rise and going of your stairs, measure the distance from the top of the decking to the ground. Be sure the measurement is taken vertical from the top and not at an angle. For example, the distance might be 1200 mm.

2 Divide this measurement by 175 mm (average riser height), then round it to the nearest whole number, for example 1200 divided by 175 = 6.86 or 7 risers. Now divide 1200 by 7 to find the finished riser height (171 mm).

3 To check that this riser height is acceptable, decide on a going (275 mm is average) and use the $2R + G$ formula: $(2 \times 171) + 275 = 617$ mm, which fits the formula.

4 There is one less tread than risers (the top of the deck is not considered a tread). Therefore, in our example there would be 6 treads. The total going would be 6 x 275 = 1650 mm.

5 The length of the string forms the hypotenuse of a right-angled triangle where the other two sides are the total going and the total rise (see the diagram below). The formula is $a^2 + b^2 = c^2$, where a is the total going, b is the total rise and c is the length of the string. Therefore, in the following example, $1650^2 + 1200^2 =$ the length squared (2040.221^2). The length of the string is then rounded off to 2040 mm.

CONSTRUCTING THE LANDING PAD

6 Set out the pad. The position is determined by measuring out horizontally from the face of the deck, the total going of the stair (for example, 1650 mm). The pad will need to be a little closer to the deck (about 300 mm) so the strings rest on it. It should be a little wider than, and extend in front of, both strings (so that you can step on it), and be about 100 mm deep.

7 Excavate and place a form in the area for the pad. Pour the concrete and leave it to set for at least 48 hours. Galvanised angle brackets to

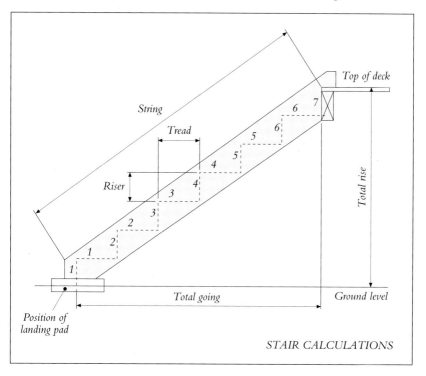

STAIR CALCULATIONS

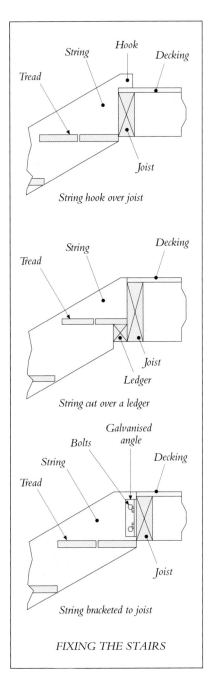

String hook over joist

String cut over a ledger

String bracketed to joist

FIXING THE STAIRS

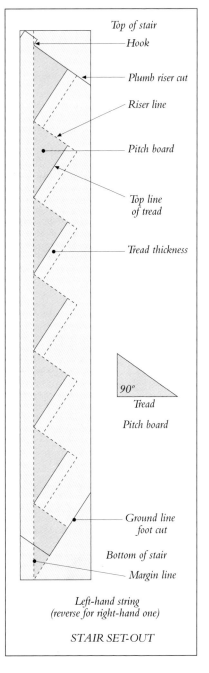

Pitch board

Left-hand string
(reverse for right-hand one)

STAIR SET-OUT

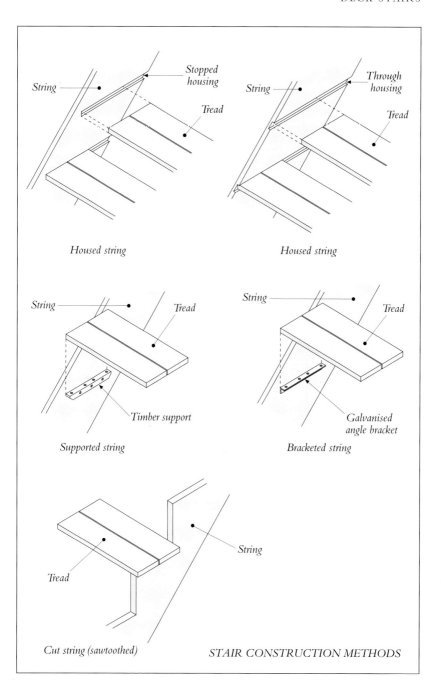

Stopped housing

String

Tread

Housed string

Through housing

String

Tread

Housed string

String

Tread

Timber support

Supported string

String

Tread

Galvanised angle bracket

Bracketed string

Tread

String

Cut string (sawtoothed)

STAIR CONSTRUCTION METHODS

hold the strings may be cast in the pad, or bolted on later.

8 Use a straight edge and level to determine the new rise height from the top of the pad. Divide the height by the number of risers (7) to find the finished height of each.

MARKING OUT THE STAIRS

9 Decide on the type of stair you want and cut a 'pitch board' template from plywood or thick cardboard, to represent one riser and one tread.

10 Cut two strings from 300 x 50 mm timber, cutting them longer than the calculation to allow for vertical cuts and hooks at the top and a level foot at the bottom (see page 44). Place the two strings side-by-side. Mark a margin line on the face parallel to the top edge (not required if a sawtooth shape is being used).

11 Start about 50 mm in from one end of the string and trace around the template, moving it along the margin line for each tread and riser. Turn the template over and repeat on the other string. At the top, mark a hook if required. Mark the thickness of the treads.

12 Cut the housings in the strings to receive the treads with a power saw or router and carefully clean out with a chisel. Alternatively, fix brackets or supports to the face of the strings, or cut the top of each string in a saw-tooth shape.

13 Cut the end of the string as required, ensuring you have a pair (one left-hand and one right-hand).

14 Cut the treads to length. Check the fit in each housing and adjust as required. Slightly round or bevel each long edge with a hand plane. Apply a water repellent or stain to housings and end grains.

15 Stairs with more than four treads may be very heavy to manoeuvre, so fix only the top and bottom treads with 75 x 3.75 mm galvanised lost-head nails or screws. The remaining treads will be fixed later.

16 Position the stairs and secure the strings to the joist at the top and the angle bracket at the bottom. The rest of the treads may now be fixed.

17 If the stair is not directly against a wall, place a number of threaded tie rods across the stair directly under the treads at 1350 mm centres maximum. Use washers and nuts on both sides of each string to hold the rods in place.

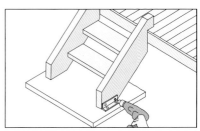

16 Position the stairs and secure the strings to the joist at the top and the angle bracket at the bottom.

DECK FURNITURE

Outdoor furniture can help you make the most of your deck. There is a large variety of ready-made timber furniture available, and you can choose timbers that match your decking material. Alternatively, you can purchase timber without a finish so you can apply one that matches your deck.

Benches can also be built as part of the deck structure. They can be fixed directly to the joist below the decking or attached to the posts around the edge of the deck (as in the diagram below). However, seating attached to the edge of the deck is not a substitute for a handrail and balustrades. The handrail should be higher behind a bench so that anyone (especially children) standing on it does not fall over the edge.

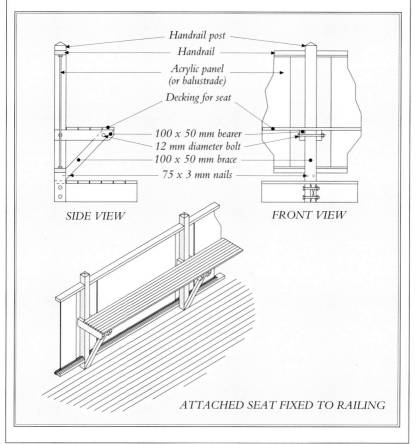

Handrail post
Handrail
Acrylic panel (or balustrade)
Decking for seat
100 x 50 mm bearer
12 mm diameter bolt
100 x 50 mm brace
75 x 3 mm nails

SIDE VIEW

FRONT VIEW

ATTACHED SEAT FIXED TO RAILING

Handrails

Handrailing can transform a plain-looking deck into an architectural masterpiece. However, it should blend in with its surroundings, as it will be the first part of the deck that people notice.

HANDRAIL REGULATIONS

In the interests of safety, any handrail must be securely fixed and built to current regulations. Check with your local authority, which will have regulations similar to these:

• Stairs over 600 mm or five risers high must have a handrail 900 mm or more above the front edge of the tread.

• Floors (decking) more than 600 mm above ground or floor level must have a handrail at least 900 mm high.

• Floors more than 3 m above ground or floor level must have a handrail at least 1 m high.

• The maximum recommended span for handrails varies according to the size of the timber used and whether there is a balustrade (see the tables opposite and on page 50).

• The maximum space between balusters must not exceed 100 mm.

• Handrails are required on both sides of stairs and ramps when these are over 1 m wide.

THE STRUCTURE

There are many handrail designs, but all must have firmly secured posts and top rails. A bottom rail and balusters usually give extra support.

In some deck designs the posts extend from the footing through the

MAXIMUM HANDRAIL SPANS (NO BALUSTRADE)

TIMBER (mm)	Max. span (mm)		
	C16	C24	OAK
170 x 25			1000
190 x 25		900	1000
70 x 35		900	1000
90 x 35	900	1000	1200
120 x 35	1100	1200	1400
140 x 35	1200	1300	1500
170 x 35	1300	1400	1600
190 x 35	1400	1500	1700
220 x 35	1500	1600	1900
240 x 35	1600	1700	2000
70 x 45	1200	1300	1500
90 x 45	1400	1500	1700
120 x 45	1600	1700	2000
140 x 45	1800	1900	2200
170 x 45	1900	2100	2300
190 x 45	2100	2200	2400
220 x 45	2200	2300	2500
240 x 45	2200	2300	2500
65 x 65	2100	2200	2400
70 x 70	2300	2400	2600
90 x 70	2500	2600	2800

A securely fixed handrail is essential for any deck more than 600 mm above the ground in order to prevent accidents. Here, lattice infill is used to give an attractive finish with an outdoor feel.

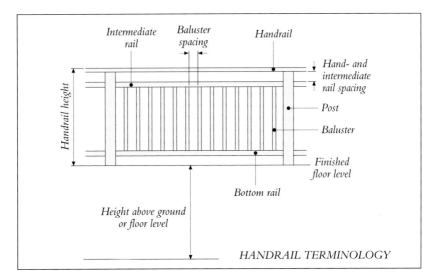

Intermediate rail · Baluster spacing · Handrail · Hand- and intermediate rail spacing · Post · Baluster · Finished floor level · Bottom rail · Height above ground or floor level · Handrail height

HANDRAIL TERMINOLOGY

MAXIMUM HANDRAIL SPANS (WITH BALUSTRADE★)			
	MAX. SPAN (mm)		
TIMBER (mm)	C16	C24	OAK
70 x 35	1700	1800	2100
90 x 35	2300	2400	2600
120 x 35	2900	3000	3300
140 x 35	3200	3400	3700
170 x 35	3400	3600	4000
190 x 35	3600	3800	
70 x 45	1900	2100	2300
90 x 45	2500	2600	2800
120 x 45	3100	3200	3500
140 x 45	3500	3600	3900
170 x 45	4000		
190 x 45	4000		

★ Provide vertical support at 900 mm centres maximum.

decking to support the handrail. This is by far the strongest method. Otherwise, handrail posts must be fixed to the joists. (The tables on page 48 and left give the maximum permissable handrail spans and, therefore, the spacings for the posts.) Note that for reasons of space, in these two tables 'oak' is a shorthand for 'hardwood'.

Timber for handrail posts should not be smaller than 70 x 70 mm or 90 x 45 mm, with a stress rating of C24. House the bottom of the post over the joist and secure it at the base with two 10 mm diameter bolts. Use a level to keep them vertical.

Handrails and bottom rails may be fixed to the face of the posts or housed into the sides and secured with galvanised nails or screws.

Balustrades are fitted between the handrail and deck or bottom rail to form a safety screen and decoration.

The handrail should blend in with its surroundings and meet the requirements of the building regulations. Some common designs are shown on page 53.

CONSTRUCTING A HANDRAIL

The handrail and balustrade are installed after the decking and stairs have been fixed.

1 Mark a level line on one end post to represent the top edge of the handrail. Transfer it to the other end post with a water level. Snap a chalk line between to transfer the height onto any intermediate posts. Trim the posts to height (this may be above or below the line depending on your design). Locate the position for the bottom rail (if required) by measuring down from the top set-out line. Square these lines across the sides of the posts and mark a 10 mm deep housing at each location to receive the rails. With some designs the rails are simply screwed or bolted to the face of the posts, and corners are either mitred or overlapped.

2 Apply a coat of preservative (stain or paint) and nail or screw the rails into their housing (see the diagram on page 52). Shaped handrails are best secured to the posts with pipe dowels and two screws from underneath to prevent the rails twisting. To prevent the bottom rail bowing down over a large span, a blocking piece is placed between it and the deck.

3 Space the balusters evenly along the railing with 100 mm maximum between them. To calculate the spacings, add the width of one baluster (say, 40 mm) to 100 mm:

40 + 100 = 140 mm

Divide the distance between the posts (say, 2000 mm) by this and round the result up to a whole number:

2000 divided by 140 = 14.28, rounded up to 15 balusters

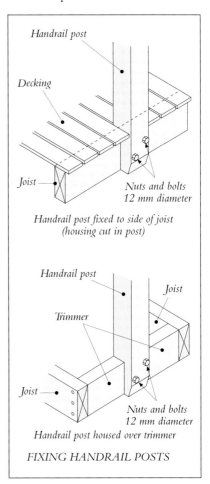

Handrail post

Decking

Joist

Nuts and bolts
12 mm diameter

*Handrail post fixed to side of joist
(housing cut in post)*

Handrail post

Joist

Trimmer

Joist

Nuts and bolts
12 mm diameter

Handrail post housed over trimmer

FIXING HANDRAIL POSTS

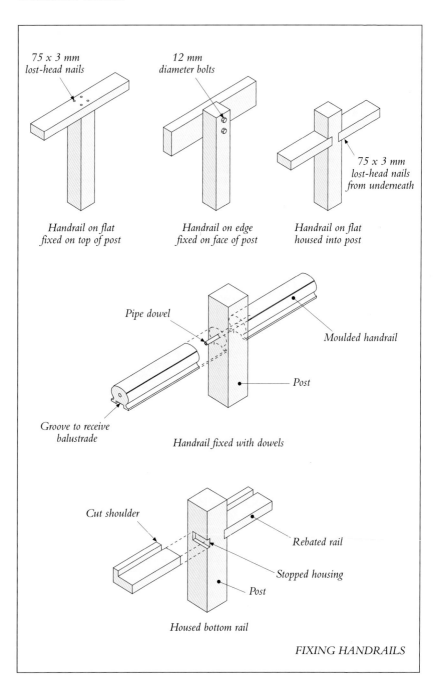

75 x 3 mm
lost-head nails

12 mm
diameter bolts

75 x 3 mm
lost-head nails
from underneath

Handrail on flat
fixed on top of post

Handrail on edge
fixed on face of post

Handrail on flat
housed into post

Pipe dowel

Moulded handrail

Post

Groove to receive
balustrade

Handrail fixed with dowels

Cut shoulder

Rebated rail

Stopped housing

Post

Housed bottom rail

FIXING HANDRAILS

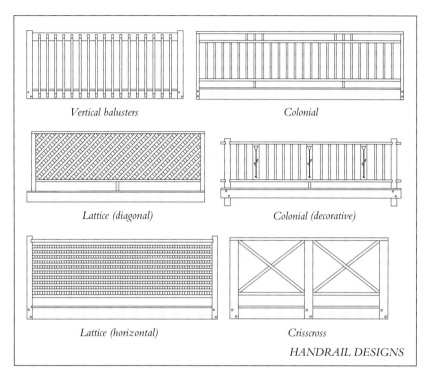

Vertical balusters

Colonial

Lattice (diagonal)

Colonial (decorative)

Lattice (horizontal)

Crisscross

HANDRAIL DESIGNS

Multiply the result by the width of one baluster:

15 x 40 = 600 mm

Subtract the result from the distance between the posts:

2000 – 600 = 1400 mm

Divide by the number of spacings required (15, one more than the number of balusters):

1400 divided by 15 = 96 mm, the required spacing

4 Cut a piece of timber to this width to act as a spacer. Place the first baluster in position with the spacer between the baluster and the handrail post, ensuring it fits neatly into any grooves or rebates on the rails.

Before fixing, check for vertical. Secure at the top and base with nails or screws. Continue to move the spacer and fix each baluster in turn. Once you are about halfway, check the gap to ensure your spacings are correct. Adjust as required.

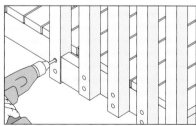

4 Move the spacer and fix each baluster in turn, securing it at the top and bottom with nails or screws.

A finished deck will need a good, protective finish in order to withstand the elements of nature.

Finishing the deck

Decks are exposed to the weather and so need to be given a protective finish. This will ensure that the timber lasts longer and the structure remains in good condition.

PROTECTING TIMBER

The surface of all exterior timber will eventually become weathered and discoloured, and even split or crack. Rot and mildew are more serious effects of weathering. To help counteract it, apply a water repellent and a finish coat of oil or paint.

• Most water repellents provide limited protection and need to be applied every six months or so. The repellent penetrates the surface of the timber without altering its natural colour, although pigments may be added. Other additives, such as ultraviolet stabilisers, insecticide and fungicides, can be incorporated for greater protection.

• Especially formulated decking stains or oils can be used for a natural look or to change the colour of the timber. Both stains and oils provide protection for up to three years, or even longer depending on the conditions. They are easy to apply and maintain and don't peel, crack or blister like some paints do. Stains will perform better when the surface has had a primer coat of water repellent.

• Any paint used should be specially formulated for external timberwork: ordinary house paint will not withstand the constant exposure to the weather. Paint manufacturers make special paint for decking.

METHOD

1 Make sure the timber is dry or the finish may blister or crack. To test, splash a handful of water across the boards. If the water is absorbed by the timber within a few minutes, the timber is dry. However, if the water remains on the surface for some time, the timber is wet and needs time to dry out before finishing. This could take up to a week or more.

2 If the timber has discoloured patches, remove them by sanding or washing the timber down with a timber bleach. To eliminate minor defects such as marks, splintering or rough surfaces, lightly sand the surface and then ensure it is free of dust or oil before finishing. Pressure-treated timber may have powdery deposits on the surface. Remove them by lightly washing the surface with mild soap and water.

3 Using a paint brush or roller, apply the finish. Keep an even amount on the surface and work the edges so that they remain wet, to avoid a streaky or patchy appearance.

Octagonal free-standing deck

This octagonal split-level deck is attractive and useful. It rests on brick piers and is built around a tree. A step is incorporated on one low side and a storage box/seat on another side.

MATERIALS

Concrete

Bricks and mortar

Damp-proof course

Capping

150 x 50 mm frame and radial joists

100 x 50 mm intermediate joists

50 x 50 mm battens

65 mm decking boards

Timber for temporary braces

Nail plates

75 mm galvanised nails

25 mm galvanised clout nails

Twisted-shank galvanised nails

TOOLS

See the basic tool kit on page 15.

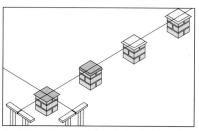

3 Align the outside of the brick piers with the string line and add damp-proofing and capping.

SETTING OUT

1 Set out the basic square shape as described on pages 18–19. For an octagon with sides 1.8 m long, start with a square with sides 4350 mm long. Make use of any slope as shown in the diagram on page 58. To locate the footing positions for the octagon, measure the diagonals and divide by 2 to find x. From each corner of the square, measure x distance along each side to find eight points a. Join point a to point a across each corner to form the octagon. To check the set-out, measure the distances from a to a around the octagon. If your set-out is correct, they should all be equal.

2 The size of deck will determine the number of footings required (see Bearer sizes on page 11). Each side of this octagon is 1.8 m and so it will require footings at each corner and one in the centre (see diagram on page 58). Add footings at corners of the original square where you want a step or storage box/seat.

3 Build footings and brick piers (see pages 21–3) with a lower pier for the step. Align them to the string line and add damp-proofing and capping.

This free-standing octagonal deck was built to cover an area below a large tree where grass would not grow. It is now a pleasant place to sit in summer.

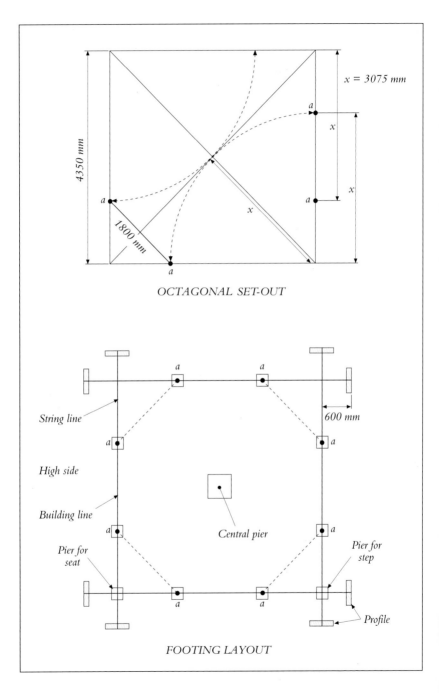

OCTAGONAL SET-OUT

FOOTING LAYOUT

OUTER FRAME

4 If you are incorporating a step, place 150 x 50 mm joists on the appropriate piers (see diagram on page 60). Use halving joints to join them and secure with nail plates. Keep each joist in line with the string line, checking with a spirit level. Check the corner for square and secure a temporary brace across the joists. Mark the position of the octagonal side in from each corner. Cut the ends of an octagonal joist at 45 degrees. Then, place it on the lower joists and fix it at either end.

The storage box has a lift-off lid that rests on the intermediate joists.

5 Cut the other joists the same way and lay them on the piers to form the octagon. If you are adding the seat at one corner, extend the joists there and join them with a halving joint. Take offcuts from the joists and fix them to the lower joists where there are two layers (at step and seat) as extra support.

INNER FRAMEWORK

6 Radial joists provide stability. Cut one joist to span from one corner of the octagon to the other, passing over the centre pier. Bevel-cut both ends to fit into the octagonal frame. Fix the joist in position with 75 x 3.75 mm galvanised lost-head nails.

7 Measure along this joist and mark the centre. Cut six joists to span from the other corners of the octagon to the centre line. Bevel-cut the ends to fit; fix with 75 mm galvanised nails.

8 Place two intermediate joists within each triangle so the joist of the octagonal frame is divided into

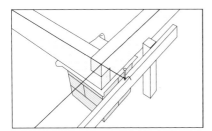

4 Use halving joints to join the joists and secure them with nail plates. Align them with the string line.

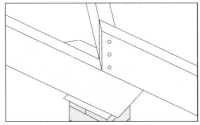

5 Cut the ends of the octagonal joists at 45 degrees and place on the lower joists. Fix off-cuts as extra support.

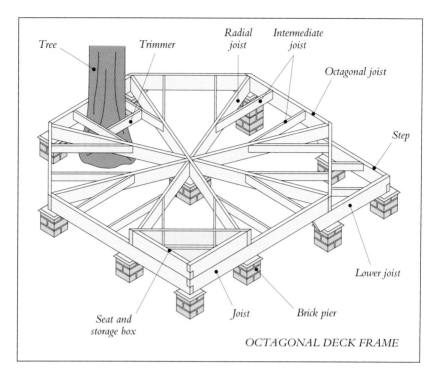

Tree · Trimmer · *Radial joist* · *Intermediate joist* · Octagonal joist · Step · Lower joist · Seat and storage box · Joist · Brick pier

OCTAGONAL DECK FRAME

three equal sections. Fix them to the octagonal frame with joist hangers. Bevel-cut the other ends, and then nail them to the radial joists.

9 Fix two intermediate joists in the step in the same way.

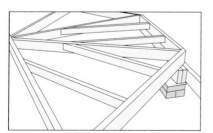

8 Put two intermediate joists within each triangle so the octagonal frame is divided into three equal sections.

10 If necessary, fix trimmers between the joists to create an opening around a tree.

11 Nail 50 x 50 mm battens to each side of all radial joists to increase the surface width. This will provide extra stability for the decking boards.

12 Use a straight edge to check the top ends of all joists are flush at each joint, and in alignment. Correct high spots or bowing with a power plane.

LAYING THE DECKING

13 On two adjacent radial joists, mark 40 mm in from the outside edge and stretch a string line

between these points. This is the position of the first board, allowing for a 25 mm overhang. Choose a straight decking board, slightly longer than the octagonal joist. Secure the board at one end, leaving enough of it projecting so that you can trim it later. Nail it to the intermediate joists, making sure that it aligns with the string line.

14 Scatter several boards loosely across the joists to determine the most appropriate ones to use. Cut lengths to fit the triangle as you work towards the centre. These boards will also provide a work platform. Fix each board, leaving a small gap between them (see page 37). Continue fixing boards until you reach the centre. Check the decking is parallel and straight.

15 Fix a straight edge across the face of the decking so that the trimmed ends of the boards align with the centre of the radial joists. This will act as a guide for the power saw. Cut the boards to shape. Repeat on the other side of the triangle.

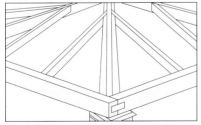

11 Nail battens to each side of every radial joist to provide extra stability for the decking boards.

16 Trim one end of the starter board for the next triangle at 22.5 degrees. Fix it in place as before, with a 25 mm overhang. Trim the ends of several more boards at the same angle and fix them in place. Keep the ends aligned with the boards of the previous section. Continue moving towards the centre, checking as you go. Repeat this procedure for the remaining sections and finish either side of the final section (the section with the tree if you are incorporating one into your deck).

17 If you are incorporating a tree, fix boards in the same way until you reach a suitable distance from the trunk (allowing the tree room to move and grow). Move to the other side of the tree. Start at the first full board away from the trunk, and continue to fix boards towards the centre. Fill in the gap either side of the tree, ensuring the space around it is maintained.

FINISHING
18 Fix fascia boards made from decking around the perimeter of the deck. Mitre the corners.

19 Fit decking boards to the step and storage box, cutting them at 45 degrees on each end. Begin at the octagonal joist and work to the corner. Use decking boards to construct a lift-off lid for the box.

20 Add a protective finish to ensure the deck stands up to weathering.

The blue and white colour scheme used on the balustrade here cleverly reflects the poolside ambience.

Pool decks

Decks can make ideal surrounds for swimming pools, as they ensure a non-slip surface that is comfortable and not too hot to walk on, even on the hottest day.

BUILDING A POOL DECK

If you have an above-ground pool or one that has been constructed on a sloping site, a timber deck is an ideal way of providing access to the water.

A pool deck is constructed in the same way as any deck, but there are a few extra points to consider:

• Prepare the ground below the deck so water will drain away. One way is to lay landscape fabric on the ground and cover it with river pebbles.

• When laying the decking boards, leave a small gap between them to allow water to drain away and prevent 'ponding' on the surface.

• As the deck will be subjected to constant splashes while the pool is in use, as well as rain, it should be constructed of timber that has been treated with a water repellent.

• For decks around salt-water pools all fittings should be of stainless steel or hot-dipped galvanised metal.

Tools for building decks

Some of the most useful tools for building decks are shown below. Build up your tool kit gradually – most of the tools can be purchased from your local hardware store.

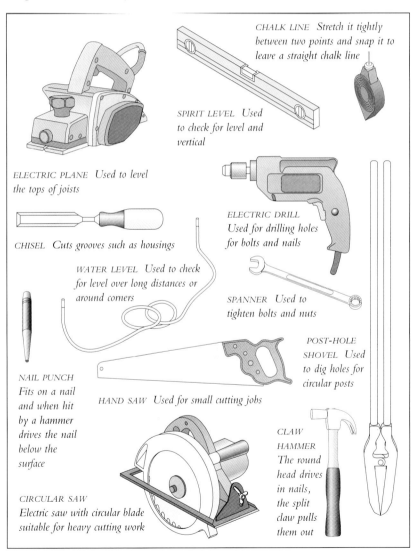

CHALK LINE *Stretch it tightly between two points and snap it to leave a straight chalk line*

SPIRIT LEVEL *Used to check for level and vertical*

ELECTRIC PLANE *Used to level the tops of joists*

CHISEL *Cuts grooves such as housings*

ELECTRIC DRILL *Used for drilling holes for bolts and nails*

WATER LEVEL *Used to check for level over long distances or around corners*

SPANNER *Used to tighten bolts and nuts*

POST-HOLE SHOVEL *Used to dig holes for circular posts*

NAIL PUNCH *Fits on a nail and when hit by a hammer drives the nail below the surface*

HAND SAW *Used for small cutting jobs*

CLAW HAMMER *The round head drives in nails, the split claw pulls them out*

CIRCULAR SAW *Electric saw with circular blade suitable for heavy cutting work*

Index